A Little Monster's

GUIDE TO MINDFULNESS

An Hachette UK Company
www.hachette.co.uk

Vie Books, an imprint of Summersdale Publishers Ltd
Part of Octopus Publishing Group Limited
Carmelite House
50 Victoria Embankment
LONDON
EC4Y 0DZ
UK

www.summersdale.com

Printed and bound in China

ISBN: 978-1-80007-723-2

Substantial discounts on bulk quantities of Summersdale books are available to corporations, professional associations and other organizations. For details contact general enquiries: telephone: +44 (0) 1243 771107 or email: enquiries@summersdale.com.

Neither the author nor the publisher can be held responsible for any loss or claim arising out of the use, or misuse, of the suggestions made herein. None of the views or suggestions in this book are intended to replace medical opinion from a doctor. If you have concerns about your health or that of a child in your care, please seek advice from a medical professional.

A Little Monster's
GUIDE TO MINDFULNESS

Emily Snape

Note to parents and carers

This book will help your child to:

- understand what mindfulness is

- recognize their emotions and focus their attention on what they're feeling and doing in the present moment

- ease feelings of stress and anxiety

- build key life skills like self-control

- feel calmer and happier with fun, simple mindful activities.

These approaches can become powerful tools that will encourage your child to calm themselves and slow down.

Hi!

I'm Pickle. What's your name?

We're moving house soon and I will have to go to a new school. I get a yucky, fizzy feeling in my tummy whenever I think about it.

Mr Growl (my teacher) suggested I keep a MINDFUL JOURNAL. He explained that being mindful is focusing on what's going on RIGHT NOW, instead of what HAS happened or MIGHT happen. It can help you feel better.

I'll try ANYTHING (I even ate dinner standing on my head last week).

So, here goes...

Pickle's Mindful Journal

Day of the week: Monday

What mindful activity have you tried?

I had a go at ~~medpitating!~~
~~megiatating~~
meditating.

To meditate, first you get comfy. Then you try clearing your head of worries. To do this, take slow, deep breaths.

Think about how each part of your body feels, from head to tail.

I noticed that my back felt stiff, so I relaxed it.

You can try placing a hand on your tummy, feeling it moving as you take breaths in and out.

Whoops! I dropped my journal in some mud!

Pickle's Mindful Journal

How did it make you feel?

Soooooo relaxed and flippy-floppy
until I realized...

Pickle's Mindful Journal

Day of the week: Tuesday

What mindful activity have you tried?

Mindful munching!

You can be mindful at mealtimes! Instead of eating like this...

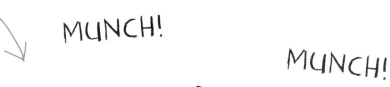
MUNCH!   MUNCH!

MUNCH!

...You slow down and enjoy each mouthful!

Pickle's Mindful Journal

How did it make you feel? Surprised.

I didn't realize bugs could be SO crunchy and slurpy AT THE SAME TIME! I loved the way the bugs wiggled in my mouth.

P.S. Children shouldn't eat bugs, so try a raisin instead! First, look closely at the wriggly skin. Give it a sniff... raisins smell great! Pop it in your mouth and feel it on your tongue. Then savour the sweet taste explosion. Yum!

Pickle's Mindful Journal

Day of the week: Wednesday

What mindful activity have you tried? Sensory play!

I tried activities using my SENSES (touch, sight, hearing, smell and taste) to help me enjoy the PRESENT MOMENT.

Mr Growl said, "ditch the screens."

Pickle's Mindful Journal

How did it make you feel? Happy!

I played a game called GUESS THE SMELL. Wearing a blindfold, you have to work out what things are by ONLY their smell. Guessing my BABY SISTER was super-easy.

Stinky

Fruity

Sweet

Zesty

Woody

Smells like monster-baby!

Pickle's Mindful Journal

Day of the week: ~~Thursday~~ Friday

Whoops, that was a loonnngg sleep.

What mindful activity have you tried?

Mindful bedtime.

Sometimes it's tricky to get to sleep, so I have been working on a mindful bedtime ritual.

I take deep breaths and imagine my worries floating away like bubbles.

I put lavender under my pillow to help me relax and it smells lovely.

Pickle's Mindful Journal

How did it make you feel?

I woke up feeling gggggrrrreat and FULL
of energy!

I think about how warm
and soft my blanket feels.

Pickle's Mindful Journal

Day of the week: Saturday

What mindful activity have you tried?

Mindful walking.

I went for a MINDFUL walk, focusing on using my SENSES and enjoying everything around me! I crunched leaves, sucked a blackberry and then lay down on the grass and did some CLOUD WATCHING.

Pickle's Mindful Journal

How did it make you feel? Peaceful.

I spotted clouds that looked like slime doughnuts, crocodiles and monster skates... three of my favourite things!

Pickle's Mindful Journal

Day of the week: Sunday

What mindful activity have you tried?

Managing my feelings by COUNTING breaths.

I found out I'm going to be sharing a bedroom with my sister which made me MAD.

Pickle's Mindful Journal

How did it make you feel? Calmer.

So, I tried taking long, deep breaths and counting to ten slowly.

Then I realized it might not be so bad. We might even get a bunk bed!

Pickle's Mindful Journal

Day of the week: Monday

What mindful activity have you tried?

Mindful kindness!

You find a friend and give each other as many compliments as you can in three minutes.

You're sooo funny!

You have an amazing ROAR!

You make great slime doughnuts!

I like hanging out with you.

Pickle's Mindful Journal

How did it make you feel? Amazing!

Pickle's Mindful Journal

Day of the week: Tuesday

What mindful activity have you tried? Mindful hugs!

It turns out you can even hug mindfully!
Hug for at least five seconds and pay
attention to how you FEEL.
Then ask the person
you hugged how
the hug made
them feel.

Pickle's Mindful Journal

How did it make you feel? Warm and cosy!

MONSTER HUG!

Pickle's Mindful Journal

Day of the week: Wednesday

What mindful activity have you tried? Mindful making!

Making art can be a really fun MINDFUL activity. You can focus on the smell of the paint, the feel of the brush and seeing your creation unfold in front of your eyes!

My school friends!

Pickle's Mindful Journal

How did it make you feel? Creative.

I'm going to put this picture up in my new bedroom!

Pickle's Mindful Journal

Day of the week: Thursday

What mindful activity have you tried?

Mindful stretching and monster yoga!

Stretching helps you connect with your body and feel energized!

Pickle's Mindful Journal

How did it make you feel?

That I can reach for the STARS!

Even my friends had a go!

Why don't you try some of these monster moves?

Pickle's Mindful Journal

Day of the week: Fri-yay

What mindful activity have you tried?

Mindful listening! My family were busy packing up the old house, so I closed my eyes and concentrated on all the sounds I could hear.

Pickle's Mindful Journal

How did it make you feel? Full of wonder!

I was so focused on listening
that I stopped feeling worried.

Pickle's Mindful Journal

Day of the week: Saturday

What mindful activity have you tried?

A mindful memory jar.

Being with my family.

My mindful journal.

Tickly hugs with friends.

Cloud watching.

Pickle's Mindful Journal

How did it make you feel? Lucky.

I've discovered there are WONDERS in every tiny moment if you slow down to notice them.

POSTCARD

Dear Mr Growl,

Thank you for all your brilliant mindful activity ideas and suggesting I keep a journal! I feel much happier when I notice all the good things around me.

See you soon!
Love Pickle XXX

Mr Growl

Slime School

Stink City

Planet Slurp

About the Author

Emily Snape is a children's author and illustrator living in London. Her work has appeared online, on television, in shops and even on buses! She loves coffee and notebooks, and has three cheeky children, Leo, Fin and Flo, who keep her on her toes and give her lots of inspiration for stories.

You can find out her latest publishing news on Instagram at @emily_snape_illustrator.

If you're interested in finding out
more about our books, find us on Facebook
at **Summersdale Publishers**, on Twitter
at **@Summersdale** and on Instagram and TikTok at
@summersdalebooks and get in touch.

We'd love to hear from you!

Thanks very much for buying
this Summersdale book.

www.summersdale.com